REBEL GIRLS

Little Library

10+ Women who Explore

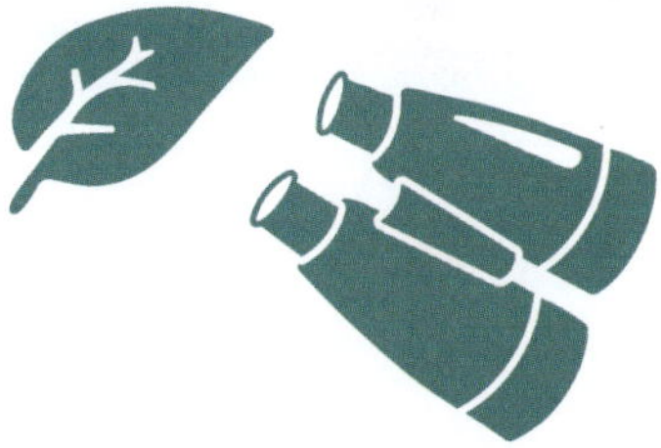

This is a work of creative nonfiction. It is a collection of heartwarming and thought-provoking stories inspired by the lives and adventures of influential women. It is not an encyclopedic account of the events and accomplishments of their lives.

www.rebelgirls.com

Rebel Girls, Inc.
421 Elm Ave.
Larkspur, CA 94939

Text by Dinah Dunn
Art direction by Giulia Flamini
Graphic design by Kristen Brittain
Graphic design and additional illustrations: Alessandro Raimondo
Portrait illustrations: 4: Giulia Flamini, 8: Amari Mitnaul,
12: Georgie Stewart, 16: Kim Holt, 20: Sarah Wilkins,
24: Kathrin Honesta, 28: June Tien, 32: Martina Paukova,
36: Maliha Abidi, 40: Geraldine Sy

Printed in China, 2023
10 9 8 7 6 5 4 3 2 1
ISBN: 979-8-88964-076-9

FSC
www.fsc.org
MIX
Paper | Supporting responsible forestry
FSC™ C018179

CONTENTS

Amelia Earhart

Aviator

July 24, 1897–July 2, 1937 | USA

The first time Amelia went to an air show, she thought airplanes were kind of boring. But two years later, a pilot took her up in the air. The world was a totally different place up there. "By the time I had got two or three hundred feet off the ground," she said, "I knew I had to fly."

Not many women at that time were pilots. But that didn't stop Amelia. She learned how to fly. She saved money to buy a yellow airplane she called the "Canary." A few years later, she became the first woman to fly across the Atlantic Ocean. She made the trip with two men.

That was exciting, but Amelia wanted to do it on her own. She trained nonstop until she was ready.

She took off in secret from Canada. She flew east over the ocean. Her tiny plane had to fly through strong winds and icy storms.

After almost 15 hours of flying, she spotted a place to land. She landed in a wide-open field in Northern Ireland with a *CLUNK*. She scared the cows but wowed the farmers. Once the world found out about her flight, she was a hero!

Amelia broke more records for flying. When she turned 40, she decided she was ready to be the first woman to fly around the world. She took only a small bag with her. Most of the space had to be used for gas for the plane.

Amelia's long flight was going well until the weather got cloudy. It was hard for her to see tiny Howland Island, where she was supposed to land. Her plane was lost somewhere over the Pacific Ocean. Sadly, it was never found.

Before leaving, she wrote that she knew the trip was dangerous. "I want to do it because I want to do it," she wrote. "Women must try to do things as men have tried."

SCAN TO HEAR MORE!

Barbara Hillary

Nurse and Adventurer

June 12, 1931–November 23, 2019 | USA

Barbara was a curious kid. And she was not much different as a grown-up. After working for 55 years as a nurse, she was ready for an adventure.

Barbara's first trip? She went to Canada in the middle of winter. There, she photographed huge polar bears. She learned how to dogsled across frozen fields. She loved the snow and ice.

When she got home, Barbara learned that no Black woman had ever reached the North Pole. She decided she would be the first. It didn't matter that she had been sick with lung cancer. Or that she didn't have the money for the trip. Or that she didn't know how to ski.

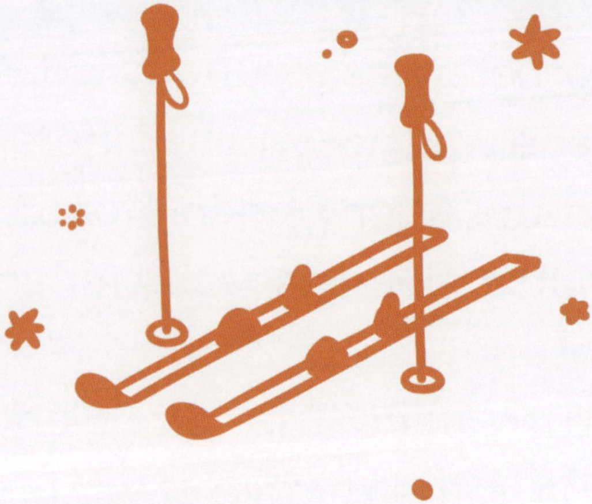

Barbara ran miles and lifted weights at the gym. She took skiing lessons and raised money for supplies. Soon she was ready to go!

Barbara took two bumpy helicopter rides to get close to the North Pole. Then 75-year-old Barbara started skiing. The gear she carried was heavy. The trip was longer and colder than any she'd made before. But she kept going.

When she reached the North Pole, she was so excited. She screamed and jumped up and down. She'd made it to the top of the world!

And she wasn't done exploring yet. Right before her 80th birthday, Barbara arrived at the South Pole. To celebrate, she drank a chocolate milk. Her curiosity took her all over the world. She loved every minute of it!

Bernice Notenboom

Climate Journalist and Filmmaker

Born June 1, 1962 | The Netherlands

As a baby, Bernice was always climbing out of her playpen. This brave little girl would grow up to be an explorer. She wrote about her trips in *National Geographic* magazine. But when she was 45 years old, a trip to the North Pole changed her life.

There are a lot of reasons not to go to the North Pole. It is a difficult trip. Freezing wind blows across your face. Ice moves around under your feet. Explorers have to pull all of their food and supplies in sleds. Also, you never know when you'll run into a hungry polar bear. But Bernice went anyway.

As she walked across the frozen ground, she saw water where there should have been thick ice.

In many places, the ice was so thin that Bernice's group couldn't move forward. They got stuck miles from the Pole without enough food. All around them, cracks in the ice were wide and deep. *This must be caused by climate change!* Bernice realized.

After they had been rescued, Bernice decided she had to do something. She traveled to places affected by climate change and told their stories. She went back to the North Pole. She also went to the South Pole, Siberia, and Greenland. She wrote books and helped make movies that showed how badly the Earth needs help.

Now Bernice travels not for adventure but to help save the world.

She brings people who have the power to change things with her. Once they see the damage, they never think about climate change the same way again.

Motorcyclist

Circa 1911–February 16, 1993 | USA

Once upon a time, a young woman named Bessie received the most amazing gift: a motorcycle. She was 16 years old. Some people in her town thought the motorcycle wasn't ladylike. *That's not how nice girls get around,* they said. Bessie didn't listen to their talk and jumped on her bike. *VROOM!* Her engine let out a mighty roar as she rode away.

Bessie loved to ride. She would pull out a map, close her eyes, and flip a penny. Wherever it landed, Bessie went. Her hair flew out from beneath her helmet as she made her way around the country. She visited 48 states in total.

But at that time, it was not safe for a Black woman to travel on her own.

On the road, Bessie couldn’t sleep in motels or eat at any diner she passed. Instead, Black families in the towns she visited took her in. Sometimes she slept on her bike under the stars. “I had my ups and downs,” she said.

In her lifetime, Bessie owned 27 motorcycles. Each one had a story. With one, she performed a stunt known as the wall of death. She would race around the inside of a giant metal globe, even riding upside down! On another, she delivered important documents during World War II. And she rode another in the Orange Blossom Parade in Miami, Florida, where she lived for years.

People called Bessie the Motorcycle Queen of Miami. Even as an 80-year-old woman, she rode her blue motorcycle to church. After her death, 200 Black women on motorcycles rode down that street, which was renamed for Bessie.

Cholita Climbers

Mountaineers

Formed in 2015 | Bolivia

Lidia Huayllas and her friends lived at the foot of a beautiful mountain in Bolivia. They were members of the Aymara people. Their families had lived in these mountains for hundreds of years. The men helped mountain climbers get to the top safely. The women, wearing brightly colored clothes and big black hats, cooked for them.

All Lidia's life, the Aymara women watched as climbers put on their helmets, backpacks, and boots. They saw the climbers' excitement as they looked up at the peak. And they waved goodbye as their men set off.

"What do you do up there?" Lidia asked her husband one day. "How does it feel?" He said she should see for herself. So that's what she decided to do.

The women pulled on their boots under their long, colorful skirts, called *polleras*. The men laughed. "You can't wear polleras," they said. "You have to wear climbing gear."

"We can wear what we like," Lidia said, strapping on her hard hat. "We are the cholita climbers!" Cholitas are young Indigenous women from Bolivia—like Lidia and her friends.

The women set off. The climb was difficult. When they reached the top of the mountain they had been looking at for years, they cried. They loved it!

Through snowstorms and strong winds, the 14 women keep climbing. Sometimes they have to start in the middle of the night to reach the top in daylight. "You're almost able to touch a star when you come up here at night!" one said.

As you read this, they are probably climbing up some rocks. The wind is blowing their multicolored skirts. And they are filled with the excitement of seeing the world from yet another peak.

Grace O'Malley

Pirate

Circa 1530–1603 | Ireland

Once upon a time, on a wild green island, there lived a girl with long red hair. Her name was Grace. When wind blew and waves crashed on the rocks, Grace dreamed of sailing across the stormy seas.

Girls cannot be sailors, her father told her. *And anyway, your long hair would get tangled in the ropes.*

Grace didn't like that one bit. She cut her hair short and dressed in boys' clothes. She would prove to her family that she could live the life of the sea.

Finally, her father agreed to take the 11-year-old sailing. But it could be dangerous. He told her, *If we meet a pirate ship, hide*. In the 1500s in Ireland, pirates often attacked ships to steal their goods.

But when pirates pulled up on their ship, Grace did not run away. She jumped from the ropes and landed on a pirate's back! She helped scare the pirates off.

Grace learned to sail but didn't want to spend her days fishing. She wanted to be a pirate! She soon had her own fleet of ships. Grace sailed as far away as Spain. She became rich by making ships pay to sail in "her" waters. She also captured a number of islands and castles along the coast.

The English navy tried to stop her. They attacked her family's castle and took her

lands. So she escaped to the sea. But then the English arrested her youngest son, Tibbott.

So Grace made the trip to meet Queen Elizabeth I to try and save him. To everyone's surprise, the English queen agreed to meet with the pirate queen of Ireland. They even came to an agreement. Elizabeth returned Grace's son and lands. And Grace returned to her home on the sea.

SCAN TO HEAR MORE!

Gunjan Menon

Filmmaker

Born December 27, 1992 | India

Gunjan grew up in a crowded city in India. But she dreamed of living deep in the forest. She wanted to tell the stories of the unusual animals that lived there.

Gunjan also acted in television shows as a child. When she was on set, she was curious about the people directing the cameras. *How did the show get put together?* she wondered.

When she grew up, Gunjan decided to she wanted to combine her interests in filmmaking and animals. She went to school to learn how to do it well.

Gunjan then followed her dream to the Himalayas. She wanted to film a red panda, her favorite animal.

There were not many left in the wild. She stayed with Menuka Bhattrai, a young woman who worked with a group to keep the pandas safe from hunters in the jungle. They were known as Forest Guardians.

Every few days, the pair got up early to walk four hours into the mountains. The weather was terrible. The ground was rocky and hard to walk on. They would sometimes find leeches stuck on their skin. Gunjan was so tired that she almost went home. But who else would tell the story of these creatures?

At Menuka's house one day, Gunjan got a call. Another Forest Guardian had spotted a red panda! Gunjan and her team quickly gathered their gear.

They were so excited that they made the four-hour hike in half the time.

At last, Gunjan spotted the red panda. She wanted to scream with joy, but she kept quiet. The red panda looked straight into her eyes. Gunjan smiled. She had the perfect shot for her film.

Through her movies, Gunjan and her team share stories of amazing animals and the people who protect them—just like she always dreamed.

Surfer

Born April 10, 1987 | Brazil

Once upon a time, there was a girl who liked big waves. Not the ones that you splash around in at the beach. She liked super-duper monster waves that could be ridden by only the best surfers in the world.

Not again, Maya, her mom would say as her daughter headed off to the beach. *You're always wet and cold. And everyone else surfing is a guy!*

But Maya didn't care. Surfing was all she wanted to do. *And as for the guys, well, they'd better get used to me!* she said.

With each wave, Maya got better at surfing. As a teenager, she started traveling the world in search of the biggest waves possible: Australia, Hawaii, Portugal, and beyond. Maya would jump on a plane and go anywhere to catch the next big one.

She won every major surf competition. She became the highest-paid big wave surfer in the world. People called her the "Super Woman of Surfing."

But one day, while Maya was surfing in Portugal, a wave caught her by surprise. The wall of water crashed over her, dragging her underwater. She broke bones and almost drowned. Luckily, her partner rescued her.

After being hurt so badly, some people would have been afraid to go back in the water. But not Maya. As soon as she healed, Maya went right back to the same beach in Portugal.

In 2020, she rode a wave that was 73.5 feet high, which is taller than a seven-story building. It was the highest ever for a female surfer. “I had never felt that energy and that noise,” she said when she was done. “It felt really terrifying.” But it was worth it.

SCAN TO HEAR MORE!

Nora Al Matrooshi

Astronaut and Engineer

Born circa 1993 | United Arab Emirates

One day in kindergarten, Nora's teacher told the class they were going to the moon! She gave them paper, glue, and cardboard to make helmets and backpacks. Nora's teacher put up a tent in the middle of the classroom. It was their spaceship.

When Nora climbed in and closed her eyes, she could almost feel the spaceship blast off. Nora had lived in the United Arab Emirates (UAE) her whole life. She had never been to the moon. What was it going to be like?

When Nora and the class burst out of the tent, her classroom was different. It was dark and everything was covered in gray cloth. It looked like they had landed on the moon! Nora was hooked. She knew that when she grew up she was going to be an astronaut.

The UAE didn't have any astronauts yet, but after college, Nora started training anyway. To become an astronaut, she had to pass a lot of tests, for both her body and her mind.

As part of her training, Nora got to talk to real astronauts! It was both scary and exciting to have a chance to meet her heroes. She also had to learn how to handle what it would be like in outer space. She was spun around fast, which might happen in a spaceship. She was also taken deep underwater to practice floating. In space, there is no gravity, so astronauts float in the air around their spaceships.

When Nora got the news that she was selected to be an astronaut, she was so happy. She would be the first Arab woman astronaut ever! She went to Texas to train at NASA. There, she prepared to go up to the International Space Station. Nora is now living her kindergarten dream!

SCAN TO HEAR MORE!

Marine Biologist

Born August 30, 1935 | USA

When Sylvia was a 12-year-old girl in Florida, an ocean wave knocked her down. She slipped underwater. But she wasn't scared—she was thrilled! Ever since then, she has loved the sea.

When Sylvia began studying the ocean, there were few other women in her classes. On her first diving trip, she was the only woman on a boat with 70 men. But she didn't care.

When she became a scientist, Sylvia put together an all-women team. They lived underwater for two weeks. They studied life in the ocean like no one had before.

"Without the ocean," she said, "there would be no life on Earth. No humans, no animals, no oxygen, no plants. If we don't know the ocean, we can't love it."

Sylvia's favorite time to dive was at night. The ocean was dark. It was sometimes hard to tell if the fish were asleep or awake. "You see a lot of fish then that you don't see in the daytime," Sylvia said.

One night in 1979, Sylvia put on a special suit. It was white and gray and as big as a space suit. It had a huge helmet with four round windows so she could see. She was going where no human had gone before: the bottom of the ocean.

Six miles out, she dived deep,

where the dark is blacker than night. Guided only by the small light from her lamp, she put her foot on the ocean floor. She was more than 1,200 feet down. It was the deepest anyone had been. She spent two hours exploring.

In her life, Sylvia has spent more than 7,000 hours underwater. One thing she noticed is how much plastic is in the sea now. "We must take care of the oceans," she says. "Will you join me in a mission to protect the Earth's blue heart?"

SCAN TO HEAR MORE!

About Rebel Girls

Rebel Girls is a global, multi-platform empowerment brand dedicated to helping raise the most inspired and confident generation of girls through content, experiences, products, and community. Originating from an international best-selling children's book, Rebel Girls amplifies stories of real-life women throughout history, geography, and field of excellence. With a growing community of nearly 20 million self-identified Rebel Girls spanning more than 100 countries, the brand engages with Generation Alpha through its book series, award-winning podcast, events, and merchandise. With the 2021 launch of the Rebel Girls app, the company has created a flagship destination for girls to explore a wondrous world filled with inspiring true stories of extraordinary women.

As a B Corp, we're part of a global community of businesses that meet high standards of social and environmental impact.

Join the Rebel Girls community:

Facebook: facebook.com/rebelgirls
Instagram: @rebelgirls
Twitter: @rebelgirlsbook
TikTok: @rebelgirlsbook
Web: rebelgirls.com
Podcast: rebelgirls.com/podcast
App: rebelgirls.com/audio

If you liked this book, please take a moment to review it wherever you prefer!